What's it?

Gadgets, Objects, Machines and More

An eye-dentification puzzle book
from the editors of OWL Magazine

Compiled by Lyn Thomas

Greey de Pencier Books

Books from OWL are published in Canada by
Greey de Pencier Books,
56 The Esplanade, Suite 306,
Toronto, Ontario M5E 1A7

* OWL and the OWL colophon
are trademarks of the Young Naturalist Foundation.
Published simultaneously in the United States by Firefly Books (U.S.) Inc.
P.O. Box 1338, Ellicott Station, Buffalo, NY 14205

ISBN 0-920775-30-6

Canadian Cataloguing in Publication Data
Main entry under title:
What's it?
ISBN 0-920775-30-6
1. Picture puzzles – Juvenile literature. I. Thomas,
Lyn, 1949-   . II. Title: OWL magazine.
GV1507 .P47W48 1988   j793.73   C87-095345-1

Photography Credits:

Ron West p.3, p.4 (bottom), p.5 (top), p.6, p.8/9, p.10, p.11, p.13, p.14, p.15, p.16 (top R & L, bottom R),
p.17, p.18/19, p.20, p.21, p.22, p.24, p.25, p.28, p.29 & 30; Christian Autotte p.4 (top), p.7 (top, bottom R),
p.12, p.16 (bottom L), p.23; Roxanne Clark p.7 (top, bottom L); Bill Ivy, p.5 (bottom);
Peter Redman p.26/27.

Art Director: Wycliffe Smith
Designer: Anita Granger
Cover photograph: Peter Redman

Special thanks to Larry MacDonald
for his invaluable assistance
with the notes that end this book.

OWL Magazine
Editor: Sylvia Funston
Art Director: Wycliffe Smith

Printed in Hong Kong

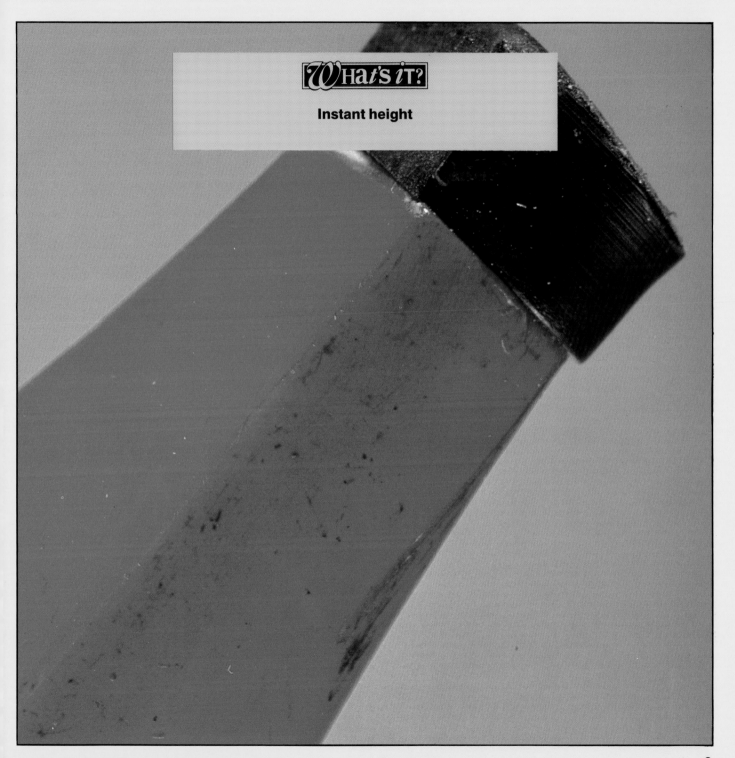

What's it?

Instant height

What's it?

1. Stick ups   2. Tooth string

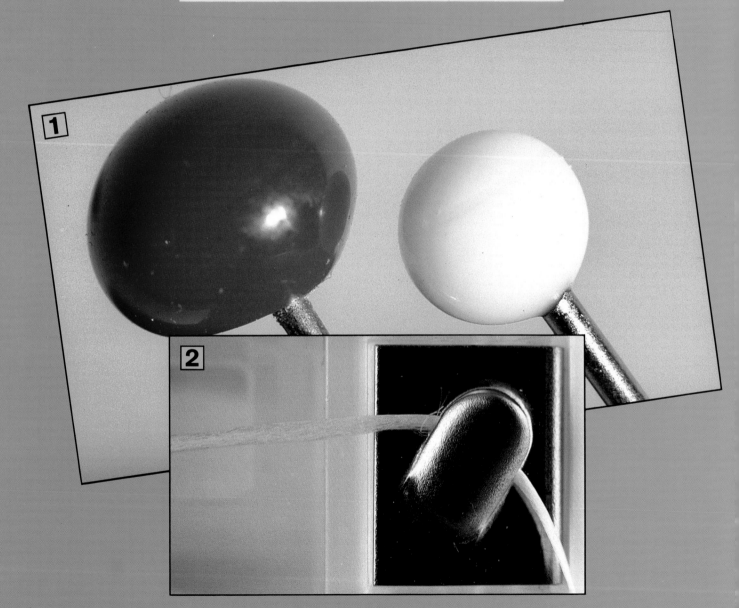

What's it?

1. Light it up if the lamp goes out

2. Happy Holidays

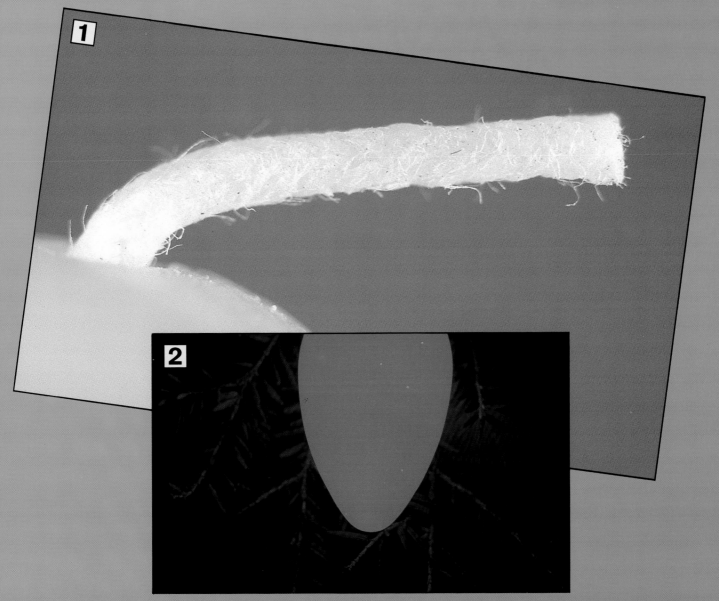

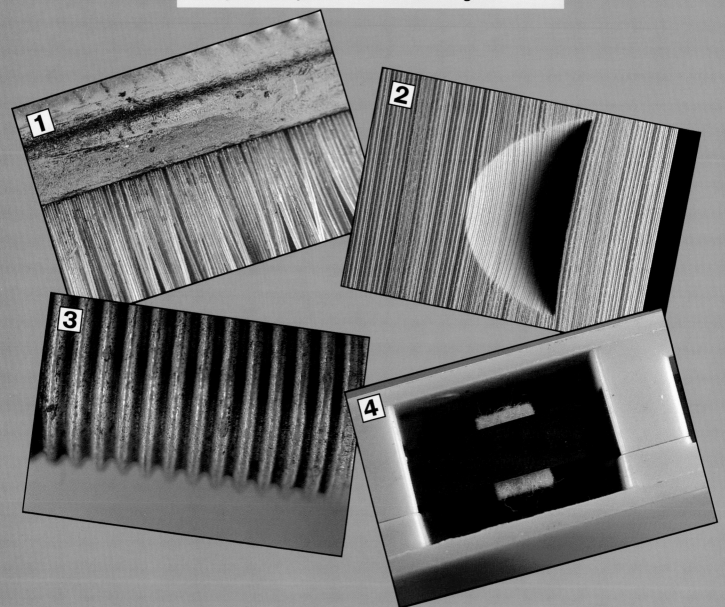

What's it?

1. Ready, set, go!
2. Tie it up
3. Use a paddle, but not a canoe
4. Shock absorbers for feet

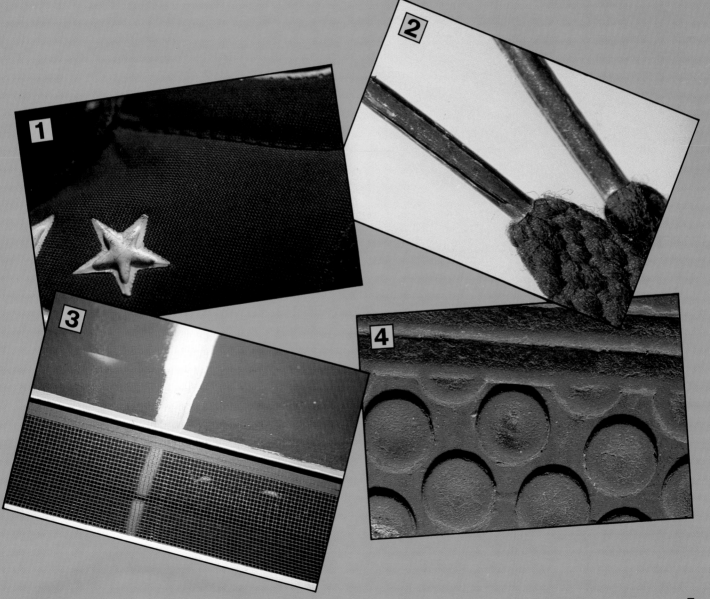

Need it when you're sick

What's it?

1. Container for beans
2. Helps to keep your pants up
3. Sew what?
4. Wind up time

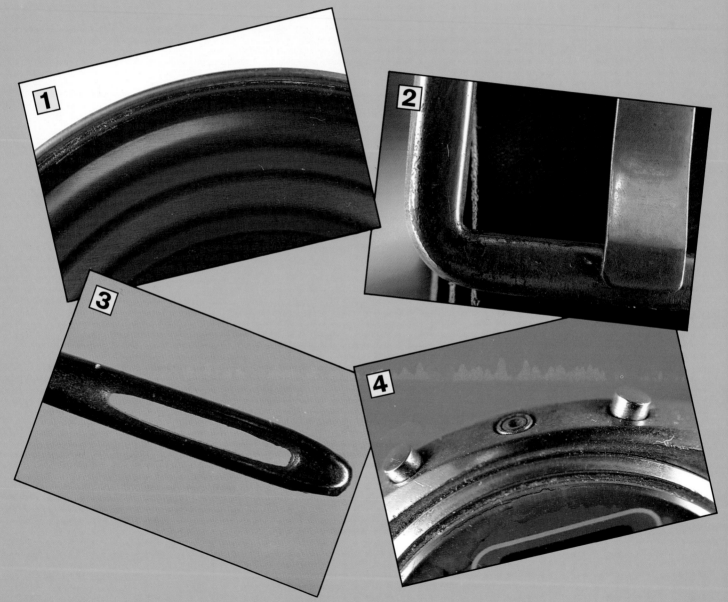

What's it?

Ouch!

1. Erasable colors   2. Groovy music

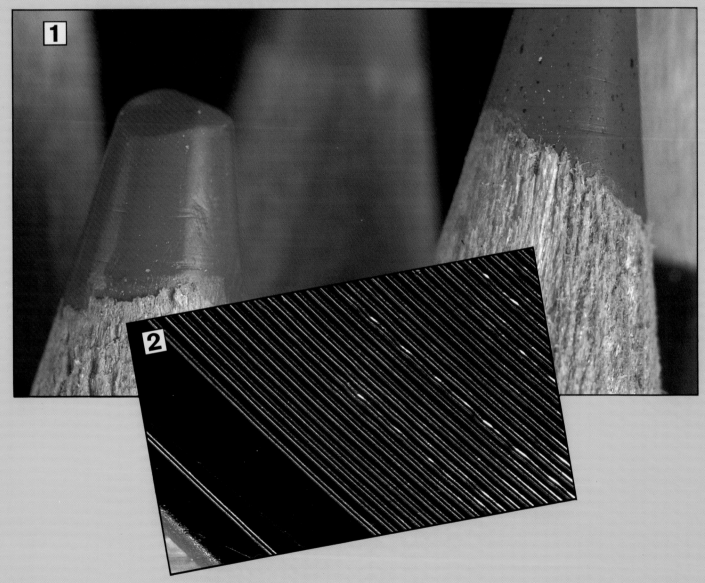

1. Writer's best friend   **2. Won't grow like your own**

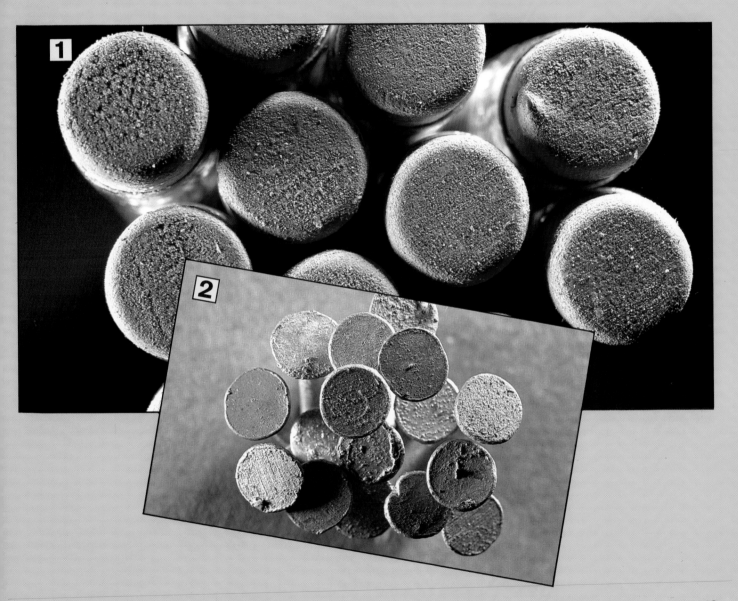

What's it?

Almost everything you buy has one on it

 What's it?

1. Is it a tie? Maybe knot!
2. A sticky roll
3. Pinch and turn
4. Don't pull too hard

15

What's it?

1. Long distance hearing aid
2. These teeth don't need toothpaste
3. A speedy fastener
4. Powerless!

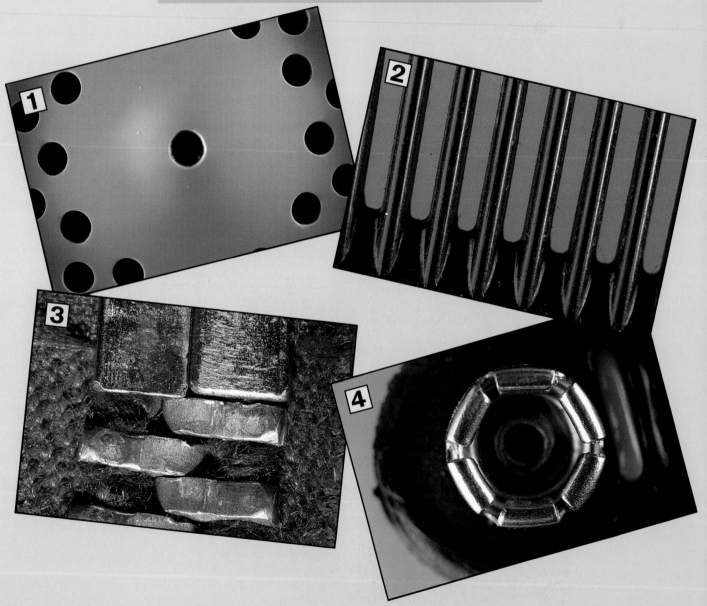

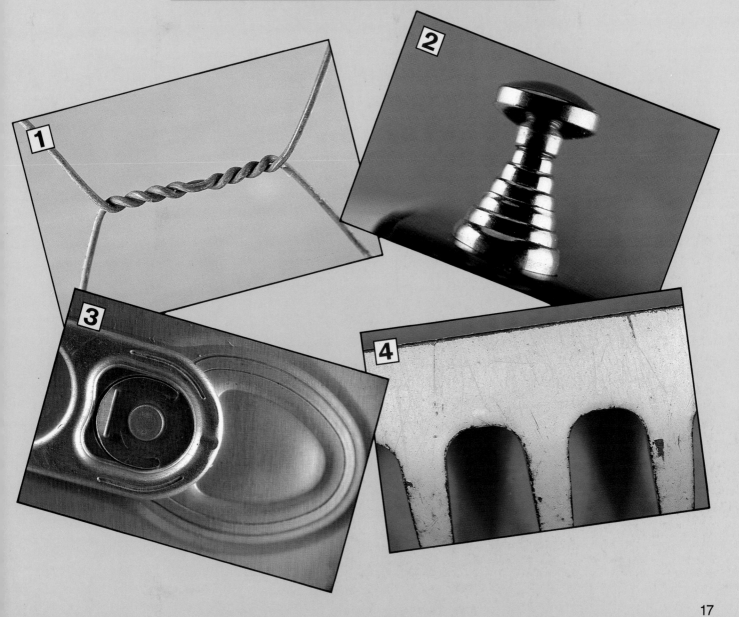

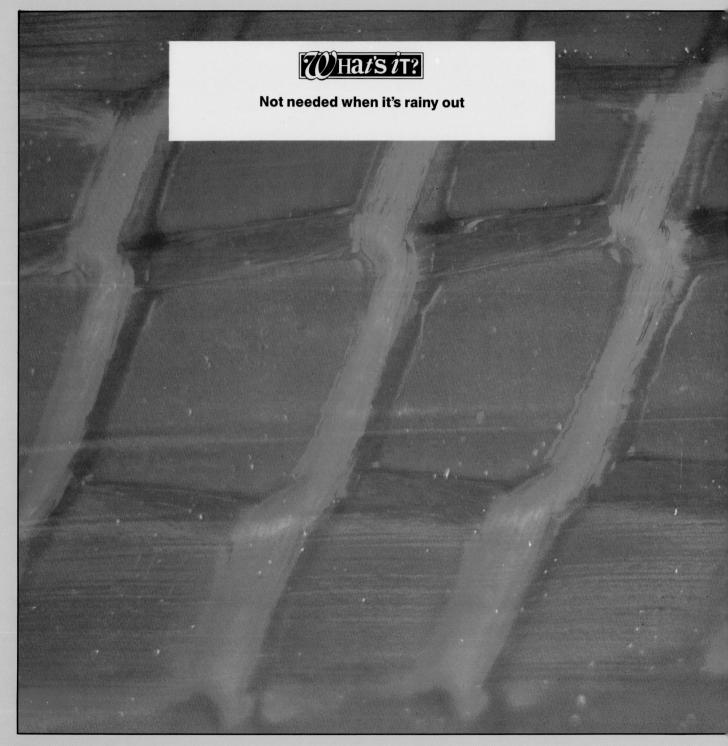

W̶Hat's iT?

Not needed when it's rainy out

What's it?

Stop it up

1. An energy line   2. Line up for water

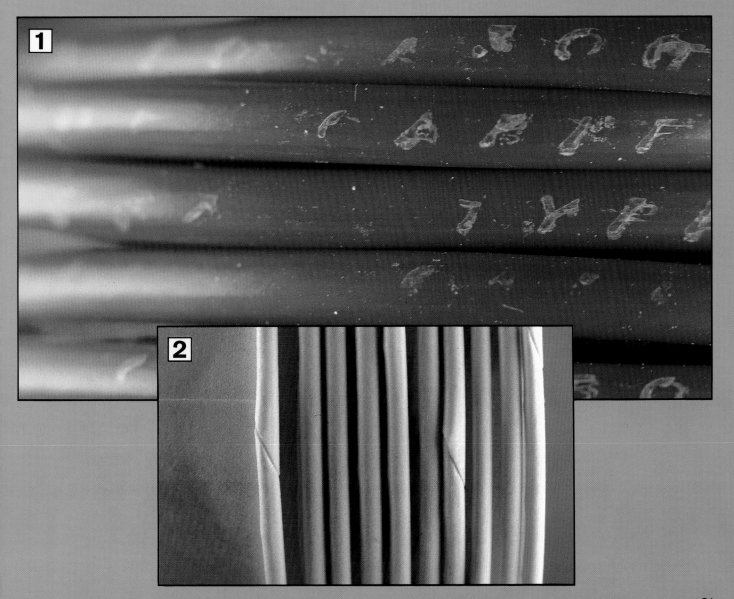

What's it?

1. Check me out
2. All hands on deck
3. Oriental squares
4. Shake, rattle and roll

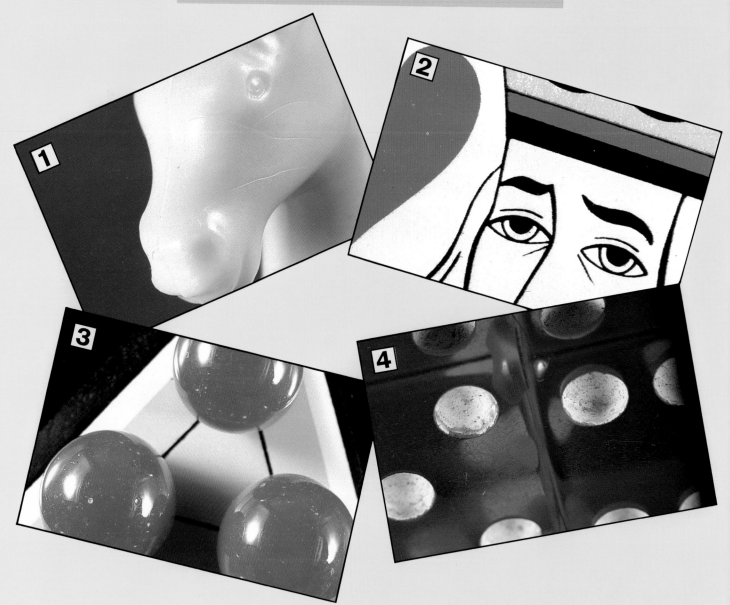

What's it?

1. Fights dirt

2. What you see on TV

*W*ha*t*'s i*t*?

Water repellent

What's it?

1. Eyes you'll find at ground level
2. Won't work if they get wet
3. Open up!
4. Food cutter

1. Gets wet to dry you
2. A soothing jelly
3. Bubble maker
4. Sparkling chompers

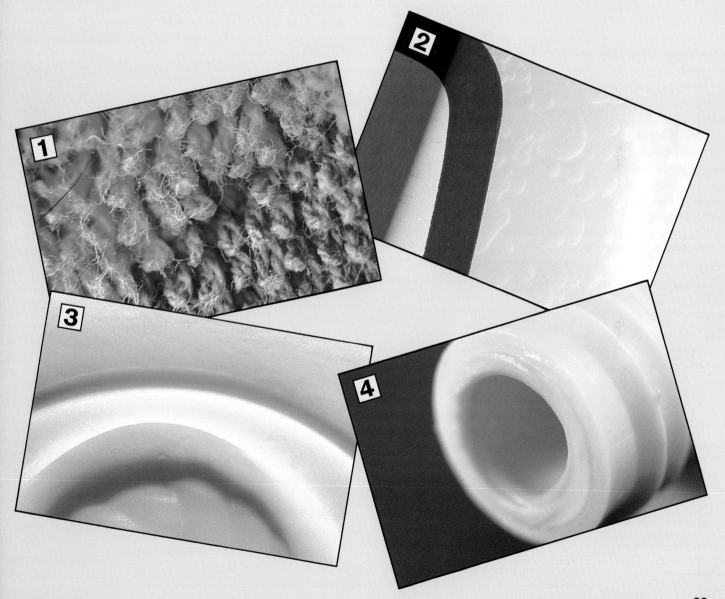

What's iT?

Jingle jangle

Answers:

PAGE 3 Shoe heel; **PAGE 4** ☐1 Pins with plastic heads ☐2 Dental floss; **PAGE 5** ☐1 Candle ☐2 Christmas tree light; **PAGE 6** ☐1 Paint brush ☐2 Dictionary thumb index ☐3 Bolt ☐4 Tape cassette; **PAGE 7** ☐1 Running shoe ☐2 Shoe lace ☐3 Ping-Pong table ☐4 Sneaker sole; **PAGE 8/9** Thermometer; **PAGE 10** ☐1 Metal can ☐2 Belt buckle ☐3 Eye of needle ☐4 Digital settings on watch; **PAGE 11** Pin heads; **PAGE 12** ☐1 Colored pencils ☐2 Record disc; **PAGE 13** ☐1 Pencils erasers ☐2 Nails; **PAGE 14** Bar code; **PAGE 15** ☐1 Spool of string ☐2 Roll of sticky tape ☐3 Twist ties ☐4 Rubber bands; **PAGE 16** ☐1 Telephone receiver ☐2 Teeth on comb ☐3 Zipper tab ☐4 Battery terminal; **PAGE 17** ☐1 Wire fence ☐2 Collapsed radio antenna ☐3 Top of soda can ☐4 Rake; **PAGE 18/19** Garden hose; **PAGE 20** Cork stoppers; **PAGE 21** ☐1 Electrical wire ☐2 Stack of paper cups; **PAGE 22** ☐1 Chess piece ☐2 Playing card ☐3 Chinese checkers ☐4 Dice; **PAGE 23** ☐1 Jeans seam ☐2 Watch band; **PAGE 24** ☐1 Laundry detergent ☐2 Dot pattern on color TV screen; **PAGE 25** Perforations on a sheet of stamps; **PAGE 26/27** Umbrella; **PAGE 28** ☐1 Shoe eyelet ☐2 Match heads ☐3 Keys ☐4 Serrated knife; **PAGE 29** ☐1 Towel ☐2 Petroleum jelly ☐3 Soap ☐4 Toothpaste tube; **PAGE 30** Stack of pennies.

Did You Know?

SHOE HEEL (page 3)
Fashion makes people go crazy! In the 1700s, some aristocratic gentlemen wore shoes with 15-cm/6-in. heels. It must have been hard to balance, let alone walk.

TAPE CASSETTE (page 6)
Next time you play your favorite 60-minute cassette tape, see if you can guess how long the tape measures. We can tell you that if you play the tape 5 hours and 50 minutes you will have listened to about 1 km/0.62 miles of tape!

DICTIONARY THUMB INDEX (page 6)
Lots of dictionaries have thumb indexes at the beginning of each new letter to help you quickly find the word you're looking for. However, the 12-volume *Oxford English Dictionary*, the largest dictionary in the world, doesn't even have one thumb index. It does, however, contain 15,487 pages, 414,825 listings, 1,827,306 illustrative quotations and 227,779,589 letters and figures. It's not the kind of reference book you use in a hurry!

SNEAKER SOLES (page 7)
Ben Johnson, the world's fastest sprinter, has been clocked at close to 37 kmh/23 mph, and was wearing sneakers at the time. How-ever, the cheetah can run about 90 kmh/60 mph — without benefit of sneakers!

THERMOMETER
(page 8/9)
Did you know that the boiling point of water varies depending on the altitude where the water is boiled? Atmospheric pressure decreases as altitude increases, and water has a lower boiling point where the air pressure is low (and a higher boiling point where the air pressure is high).

PLACE	ALTITUDE	BOILING POINT OF WATER
Dead Sea, Israel	395 m/1296 ft (*)	101°C/213.8°F
London, England	Sea Level	100°C/212.0°F
Denver, Colorado	1609 m/5280 ft (**)	95°C/203.0°F
Lhasa, Tibet	3686 m/12,087 ft (**)	87°C/188.6°F
Peak of Mt. Everest	8840 m/29,002 ft. (**)	71°C/159.8°F

* below sea level ** above sea level

You wouldn't be able to use an ordinary thermometer to measure this, though. Scientists use special thermometers to gauge extreme heat and cold.

PING-PONG TABLE
(page 7)
Ping-Pong was first played in England in the early days of the twentieth century. Although the name Table Tennis was officially adopted in 1921, most players, remembering the Ping-Pong Association founded in 1902, continued to call the game Ping-Pong, the name it is still known by today. One of the very first video games was actually a form of Ping-Pong called Pong.

METAL CANS (page 10)
No one knows exactly how many metal cans are produced throughout the world each year, but it must exceed the zillions. We do know that the best-selling canned product in the Western world is baked beans.

EYE OF NEEDLE (page 10)
The longest needle in the world is 1.86 m/6 ft. 1 in. It was crafted in England for stitching buttons onto the ends of mattresses lengthways. You'd probably have no trouble threading it — the eye must be huge.

DIGITAL SETTINGS ON WATCH (page 10)
If your watch is losing 30 minutes of time a day, when will it show the correct time again? The answer is every 24 days. But did you know that a clock that is losing just one-thousandth of a second each day will be correct only once every 118,275 years?

COLORED PENCILS
(page 12)
If you took a new lead pencil and drew a straight line along the sidewalk with it, you'd travel about 55 km/35 miles before the lead ran out. We think you'd get tired of sharpening the pencil long before you finished!

RECORD DISC (page 12)
Can you guess how many grooves there are on a long-playing record? Try just one — it's a continuous spiral groove.

PENCIL ERASERS
(page 13)
Erasers attached to the ends of pencils were first patented in the late 1950s, although erasers on their own have been around since the 1700s. The earliest erasers were first called lead-eaters and later rubbers, because they rubbed things out.

BAR CODE (page 14)
These days nearly everything you buy has a bar code on it which allows the manufacturer and the store to identify the product and price. Although not all bar codes use the same system, generally the first bars and digits are the manufacturer's

code and the next ones contain the product and price information.

RUBBER BANDS (page 15)
Just about everyone has used an elastic band as a catapult for flicking paper missiles across the classroom. Have you ever wondered how far you could pull the elastic? A rubber band can stretch to approximately four times its original length before — watch out — it snaps!

SCOTCH TAPE™ (page 15)
Adhesive tape was invented in 1925 and clear cellulose adhesive tape appeared about five years later.
When this new tape was first tested in a U.S. automobile plant, only the edges of the tape had glue on them. The workers in the plant thought this was to save glue and hence money. In those days Scotsmen were often teased for being penny pinchers who never waste anything, so the amused workers nicknamed the tape "Scotch" tape, even though it had nothing to do with Scotland. The funny nickname really stuck — and became a brand name.

TELEPHONE RECEIVER
(page 16)
Do you know why telephone buttons have both numbers and letters on them? Once, the telephone companies thought that people wouldn't be able to remember long numbers, so to make it easier, they added letters that stood for names. MA stood for MAJOR, PL for PLAZA and so on, so 621–3831 would have been MA 1–3831. Do you find it easier?
Today, the letters are sometimes used in a different way. For instance, when you're hungry, you might dial a number like 33P–IZZA, which is easy to remember as well as being great advertising for a pizza company.

ZIPPER (page 16)
The world's longest zipper measures 632.2 m/2074 ft., and has 119,007 nylon teeth. It seals the waterproof cover of underwater cables in Mendrisio, Switzerland.

COLLAPSED RADIO ANTENNA (page 17)
Sound waves travel in straight lines. That's why the sound of a car radio gets garbled when you drive under a bridge — the structure has blocked the sound waves.

TOP OF SODA CAN
(page 17)
Once, drinks that contained carbon dioxide were named pop because when the bottles were opened the corks came out with a loud "pop" — just like today's champagne bottles. The original name, soda pop, was eventually shortened to just pop.

GARDEN HOSE
(page 18/19)
Farmers use extensive sprinkler systems to water their fields, just like you use a garden hose to water your lawn. But long ago we had to rely on people or animals to carry water around. Later, the ancient Egyptians designed irrigation systems that used ditches to direct water to their fields. Farmers in some countries with little rainfall — such as in the Middle East or northern Africa — still use irrigation systems.

CORK STOPPERS (page 20)
Did you know that there was such a thing as a cork tree? Well, there is, and commercial cork, used in bottle corks, for instance, is obtained from its outer bark.

CHINESE CHECKERS
(page 22)
Chinese checkers is a variation of a game called Halma, which was developed in Greece around 1880. As its name suggests, the game found its way to Europe from China, probably with sailors or travellers.

CHESS (page 22)
Living chess, which uses real people as the chess pieces, is still played regularly in the town square of Marostica, Italy. The game is a yearly re-enactment of one in 1454, when two suitors in love with the same girl competed for her hand in marriage.

CARDS (page 22)
Your deck of playing cards contains 52 cards, although as many as 78 cards have made up a pack while the deck developed over the centuries. Hundreds of games are played with a pack of cards and some people even claim that they can tell your fortune by "reading your cards."

DICE (page 22)
According to experts, the most likely number you will get when you throw two dice will be seven. The odds of getting this are one in five times. The next most likely throw would be a six or an eight.

WATCH BAND (page 23)
When Torontonians and New Yorkers are eating breakfast at 8:00 a.m., Londoners (England) are eating lunch at 1:00 p.m., Muscovites (Russia) are drinking a quick cup of tea at 3:00 p.m. and Djakartans (Indonesia) are sitting down to dinner at 8:00 p.m. And people in Wellington, New Zealand, should be fast asleep — it's one in the morning.

JEANS SEAM (page 23)
Most of you wear denim jeans that are blue, but until 1896 they were also made from brown fabric. Oscar Levi Strauss used leftover brown tent canvas to make the first jeans, for miners. When tent canvas was in short supply he ordered a new fabric from Nîmes, France. The cloth from Nîmes (de Nîmes) soon became known as denim.

TV SCREEN (page 24)
The number of colored dots or stripes you see on your TV screen affects the clarity and sharpness (resolution) of the picture you see. For instance, having lots of thin, vertical stripes on your TV screen gives a higher resolution, whereas a screen with thicker but fewer vertical stripes means a less clear picture. And not all TVs have vertical stripes. Some have dots, some have horizontal stripes, some have mixtures of horizontal and vertical stripes and some mix dots and stripes. Switch on your TV and see which it has.

TOWEL (page 29)
Fortunately for you, most towels can sop up lots of water when you need to dry yourself, but how much water the towel absorbs depends on the kind of towel you use. A fluffy towel with a good fiber content will absorb about four times its own weight in water before it reaches saturation point. That's close to 1.5 kg/3.5 lbs. of water, or a lot more than you'll have on you when you step out of the bath.
How heavy a towel would you need to absorb all the water in your bathtub? (Hint: an average bathtub holds about 136 kg/300 lbs. of water.)

TOOTHPASTE (page 29)
Have you ever wondered how much toothpaste is inside an average tube? We can tell you that a 100-ml/3.5-fl.oz. tube contains close to 2 m/6 ft. of squeezed-out paste. So if you clean your teeth three times a day, and use about 2.5 cm/1 in. each time, a tube should last you about 25 days!

STACK OF PENNIES
(page 30)
It would take about 7 million pennies stacked one on top of the other to match the height of Mount Everest. That's a *lot* of saving.